An Animal Alphabet

Here on Earth

Written and Illustrated
by Marcia Perry

Pomegranate **kids**®
Portland, Oregon

Published by PomegranateKids®,
an imprint of Pomegranate Communications, Inc.
19018 NE Portal Way, Portland OR 97230
800 227 1428 | www.pomegranate.com

Pomegranate Europe Ltd.
Unit 1, Heathcote Business Centre, Hurlbutt Road
Warwick, Warwickshire CV34 6TD, UK
[+44] 0 1926 430111 | sales@pomeurope.co.uk

To learn about new releases and special offers from Pomegranate, please visit www.pomegranate.com and sign up for our e-mail newsletter. For all other queries, see "Contact Us" on our home page.

Library of Congress Cataloging-in-Publication Data

Perry, Marcia.
 Here on Earth : an animal alphabet / by Marcia Perry.
    pages cm — (Pomegranate catalog ; no. A217)
 Audience: Pre-school, excluding K
 ISBN 978-0-7649-6452-7 (hardcover)
 1. Animals—Juvenile literature. 2. English language—Alphabet—Juvenile literature. 3. Alphabet books. I. Title.
 QL49.P384 2013
 590—dc23
                              2012037971

Pomegranate Catalog No. A217
Designed by Ronni Madrid

Printed in China
22 21 20 19 18 17 16 15 14 13   10 9 8 7 6 5 4 3 2 1

Here on Earth

Alligators are awesome.

Ants are amazingly abundant.

Aardvarks are amusingly awkward.

Beautiful Butterflies,

big, brawny, brown Buffaloes,

Bumblebees, and Blue-footed Boobies are born.

Cozy Cats curl up comfortably.

Chameleons change colors constantly.

Crimson Cardinals catch curious Caterpillars.

Here on Earth . . .

Dazzling Dragonflies dance.

Dandy Ducks dawdle in the drink.

Delightful Dolphins dive in the depths.

Ermines are elegant.

Emus have exquisite eggs.

Elephants are enormously excellent.

We find flying Fish,

funny Frogs, furry Foxes,

and finely feathered Flamingos.

Here on Earth . . .

Geese glide gracefully.

Green Geckos grip the grass

while Giraffes and Grasshoppers graze.

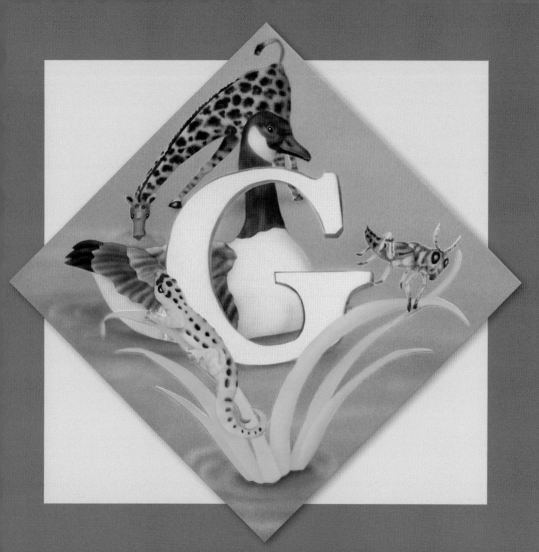

Handsome Herons

hitchhike on hospitable Hippos.

Happy Hummingbirds hover on high.

Impressive Ibises inspire.

Inquisitive Iguanas investigate.

And innocent Inchworms immigrate.

Here on Earth . . .

Jovial Jays are jabbering.

Joyful Jerboas are jumping.

Jaguars are enjoying their jungles.

We get to know

Kookaburras and Koalas,

Kiwis and Kangaroos and their Kids.

Ladybugs live on the land,
like Lemurs, Llamas, and Lions.
Lovely Loons live on lakes and lagoons.

Here on Earth . . .

Mice munch on morsels.

Monkeys make magnificent mothers.

Mysterious Moths meander in the Moonlight.

Narwhals and Nautili,

Nudibranchs and Needlefish,

navigate the ocean's neighborhoods.

Otters and Octopi

occupy the open oceans.

Owls are often found in old Oak trees.

Here on Earth . . .

Every pretty Panda,

perky Puffin, plucky Parrot,

and patient Penguin is precious.

Quails are queenly
with their chick quartets.
Quetzals have exquisite quills.

Roadrunners race.

Rabbits romp and Ravens rave.

Raccoons rummage for refreshments.

Here on Earth . . .

Slow Snails stick to Stones.

The Sun shines on shimmering Sea Stars.

Splendid Swans swim past spunky, sunning Seals.

Turtles are travelers.

Toucans take to tropical trees.

Tigers take up as much territory as they please.

Every Urchin is unique.

Umbrella Birds are uncommon.

Unicorns, though unreal, are very common.

Here on Earth . . .

The various Vipers,

the vulnerable, velvety Voles,

and the vigilant Vultures are all vital.

Woodpeckers whittle wood

while wild, woolly Wolves wander

and Whales and Walruses wallow in water.

Like the exquisite Xenops bird,

exceptional and exotic animals exist everywhere.

But sadly, some extraordinary animals are now extinct.

Here on Earth . . .

There are Yaks,

Yellowhammers, and Yapoks

sharing this world with You and me.

Zorillas and Zebras are in Zambia.

Zebra Finches and Zebra Butterflies live in Venezuela.

Amazing animals from A to Z inhabit

every zip code and zone.

We are all here on Earth together

with our favorite pets,

the birds in the trees,

and the animals in the jungles, forests,

and deep blue seas.

Here on Earth.

About the author: Marcia Perry began her career as an artist in 1973. She also taught kindergarten for seven years. She loves kids and loves to draw, paint, and sculpt nature's creations, big and small. Her art is exhibited and licensed nationally and internationally. In 2000, she cofounded Youth Arts Collective, a lively and successful after-school art studio and mentorship program for teens and young adult artists in Monterey, California, where she is living happily ever after! To see more of Marcia's art, go to www.marciaperry.com.

Acknowledgments: My love and thanks to Meg Biddle, Celia Perry, Richard Jensen, and Jim Dultz, and to teachers everywhere, for inspiring and encouraging me to make this book.